Kids Can Crafts

FRIENDSHIP
BRACELETS

Written by Camilla Gryski

Kids Can Press Ltd.

Toronto

FOR IRENE
who makes bracelets

CANADIAN CATALOGUING IN PUBLICATION DATA

Gryski, Camilla, 1948-
    Friendship Bracelets

(Kids can crafts)
ISBN 1-55074-085-7

I. Bracelets – Juvenile literature. I. Title.
II. Series

TT829.G78 1992   745.594'2   C91-095550-6

Kids Can Press Ltd.   Edited by Laurie Wark
29 Birch Avenue   Designed by Nancy Ruth Jackson
Toronto, Ontario   Electronic Assembly by Pixel Graphics Inc.
Canada M4V 1E2   Colour photography by See Spot Run
                            Printed and bound in Hong Kong
9 2 0 9 8 7 6

CONTENTS

INTRODUCTION

People have worn bracelets for thousands of years — to show their wealth or power, for luck or simply to decorate their arms. The bracelets in this book are all made by knotting threads around each other. You can make lots of different patterns using a basic knot and different arrangements of coloured threads. Embroidery thread comes in a rainbow of colours. It doesn't take much thread to make a bracelet, so knotted bracelets are both inexpensive and beautiful.

Many of the colourful knotted bracelets you see for sale today are made in Guatemala. They've come to be called Friendship Bracelets because they're often made and given by friends to friends. Some people say that they are Wish Bracelets. If you wear them until the threads break and they fall off, your wish will come true.

It's best to begin with the Diagonal Stripe Bracelet and work your way through the book. As you learn new skills, you'll be able to use more threads and try different patterns. You can mix and match bracelets, add beads and maybe even invent some designs of your own.

You and some friends can make a real friendship bracelet. Each person chooses a colour, then the bracelet gets passed around as each friend knots the row of the colour she chose.

Don't worry if you're left-handed — I'm left-handed, too. You use both hands equally when you make bracelets. Your right hand holds the knotting thread when you are knotting from the left to the right, but your left hand does all the work when you are knotting from the right to the left.

So make them for friendship or for wishes. Make them for your wrists or somebody else's. And have fun!

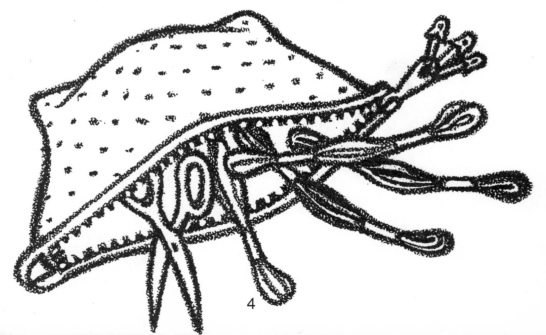

4

GETTING STARTED

You need at least four different colours of embroidery thread to make these bracelets. You can experiment with other kinds of materials — wool works if it's not too thick. You also need a pair of scissors and a safety pin to pin your bracelet to the knee of your jeans or to a pillow or cushion.

You can make a portable bracelet kit using a small bag with a zipper. Use the bag to hold your skeins of thread, the bracelet you're working on and a small pair of scissors. Keep your safety pins on the tag of the zipper so you always know where they are.

CHOOSING COLOURS

All of the bracelets in this book except the Diagonal Stripe use four different colours of thread. The Diagonal Stripe uses only three colours because it's easier to work with fewer threads when you're just learning how to make the basic knot and stitch. When you're good at keeping your threads organized, you can use more colours and make wider bracelets.

Choosing colours is lots of fun. Make a bracelet to match a favourite sweater or outfit. Use your school colours or the colours you like best. A bracelet with the blue of the sky, the orange of an Indian Paintbrush flower and the green of a pine tree can remind you of the country. Look around you to see which colours go well together. At first it's best to choose colours that are very different. You might get the order of the threads mixed up if two colours are nearly the same. Skeins that change colour from dark to light can also be confusing when you are working with pairs of threads. As you get used to working with the threads, you can create interesting patterns by choosing only two colours instead of four. You'll have to think a little harder about what you're doing, because two pairs of threads will be the same colour.

LOOKING AFTER YOUR THREADS

Skeins of embroidery thread always have a loose thread. This thread is one of the ends and if you pull gently, it will come out without tangling. You don't even have to take off the paper wrappers, so your skeins of thread will stay tidy. When the skeins of thread get skinny, the paper wrappers will fall off. Then the best thing to do is to "butterfly" the thread that's left.

TO BUTTERFLY YOUR THREAD

1. Lay one end of the thread across your palm. Let the very end dangle off the side of your hand between your thumb and index finger.

2. Put the thread between your ring finger and your little finger. Wrap the thread around your little finger.

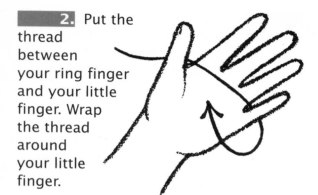

3. Now the thread goes across your palm, between your thumb and your index finger and around your thumb.

4. This is the path of the thread: Across your palm, between your ring finger and your little finger, around your little finger, back across your palm, between your thumb and index finger, and around your thumb. The threads criss-cross in the centre of your palm. You're making two sets of loops like the wings of a butterfly — one set around your little finger and one set around your thumb.

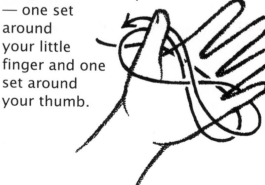

5. When you've butterflied nearly all the thread, pinch the butterfly where the threads criss-cross and lift it off your fingers. Wind the last bit of thread around the centre of the butterfly to keep it together.

MEASURING YOUR THREADS

Pick three colours of thread. Play around with the skeins to see which colours look nice side by side.

Your working threads should be about four times the length of your knotted bracelet, with some left over for the braided ends. Here's an easy way to measure. You make each working thread the length of your arm from fingertip to shoulder. Since you'll have two working threads of each colour, you measure a length of thread from your fingertip to your shoulder and back down to your fingertip again. To do this, hold the end of the thread between your thumb and index finger and measure the first length all the way up to your shoulder. Hold the thread where you've measured an arm's length and let go with your thumb and index finger. Now measure the second length, smoothing the thread down to the free end. Snip the thread. You have a piece of thread twice the length of your arm. Use this first piece of thread to measure the other two colours. You have three long pieces of thread all the same length. If you're making a bracelet for someone who's taller than you — like your dad — measure up and down his arm. The bracelet (and the working threads) will have to be longer.

TYING AN OVERHAND KNOT

1. Put one end of each colour together and smooth out the threads. Now fold the threads in half so there is a loop at the top.

2. Hold the threads in one hand and hold the loop in the other.

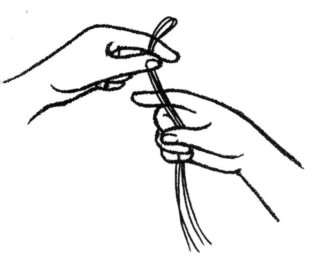

3. Wind the loop all the way around the index finger of the hand that's holding the threads. Pinch the threads together where they cross to make a circle.

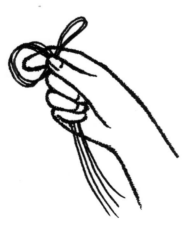

4. Hold the circle of threads together at the cross, and slip it off your index finger. Now put the free loop end of the thread through the circle and start to pull the end tight. You can move the loose knot up the thread to get a smaller loop at the top. The loop is part of the fastening of the bracelet, so you must be able to slip a braided end through it easily.

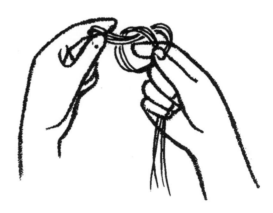

PINNING YOUR BRACELET

The loop helps to keep your bracelet firm while you work on it, so pin it securely to a cushion or your jeans. A pin works better than masking tape. Masking tape can come loose when you start tying the knots and pulling them tight.

Pin through the loop on both sides. If you just slip the pin through the loop and attach it, your bracelet will keep flipping over and you'll mix up the front and the back.

DIAGONAL STRIPE BRACELETS

You've chosen and measured your three colours. Now think about the order of your coloured stripes. If you've chosen red, yellow and blue, do you want your bracelet stripes in that order, or do you want the yellow, then the blue, then the red?

The Diagonal Stripe bracelet uses an alternating colour set-up. You arrange your threads in the order of your coloured stripes. Because you have two threads of each colour, the pattern repeats itself. Starting from the left, your threads will be red, yellow, blue, red, yellow, blue. Make a diagram that shows you the order of your colours. As you knot to make a coloured stripe, the threads will change position, but the yellow will always come after the red and the blue will always come after the yellow.

Untangle your threads right down to the ends, and spread them out like a fan. Now you're ready to start knotting.

NOTE: Remember that the threads take their numbers from their new positions, so the numbers of the threads are always changing.

THE BASIC KNOT

Number your threads in your head from left to right. 1-2-3-4-5-6. Numbers 1 and 4 are the same colour; 2 and 5 are the same; and 3 and 6 are the same.

Number 1 is your first knotting thread. You will tie two knots with number 1 on each thread all the way over to number 6 on the right.

1. Hold the knotting thread — thread 1 — in your right hand.

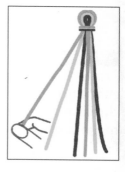

2. Pick up thread number 2 — the first base thread — with the middle, ring and little fingers of your left hand. Leave your left thumb and index finger free.

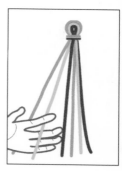

3. Make a sail shape with your knotting thread. The sail shape points to the left. The sail thread crosses over the base thread. Use your left index finger and thumb to keep the threads together where they cross.

4. Feed the end of the knotting thread up through the sail shape. Hold the base thread tight and straight, and pull the knot up to the top of the base thread.

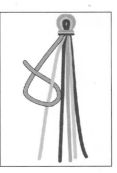

NOTE: Your knot should always be the colour of the knotting thread. If you hold the base thread loosely, and tighten your knot by pulling on both threads, your knot may be the colour of the base thread.

5. Tie another knot with thread 1 around thread 2. Make the sail shape, feed the end through, hold the base thread taut and pull the knot right up to the top. Keep the knotting thread in your right hand. You

don't need to let go of it until you've knotted all the way over to the right side. Put aside thread 2.

NOTE: Two knots on the same thread make a stitch.

6. With your knotting thread, tie two knots around thread 3, thread 4, thread 5 and thread 6. Remember the order of your colours, and don't let your work flip over.

You've made one diagonal stripe. Thread 1 is now thread 6 — it's over on the right side. You have a new knotting thread over on the left side. It's thread 1 now.

7. Pick up your new knotting thread — thread 1 — in your right hand. Remember you can hang on to it until you've finished knotting over on the right. Start your next stripe by making two knots with your knotting thread on each thread from left to right — threads 2, 3, 4, 5 and 6. The thread on the left is always thread 1. The thread on the right is always thread 6.

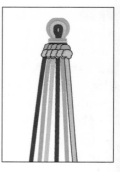

Pull each knot in this second row quite tightly. You want each knot to be tucked up against the stitches in the first row. When you've completed a couple of rows, the knots will keep the threads apart and you'll be able to see which thread comes next in the knotting order.

The fourth row will start to repeat the colour order. If your first row was red and you have three colours, the fourth row will be red too.

8. As you knot your bracelet, always remember to start with the thread on the left, and tie two knots on each thread all the way over to the right.

BRAIDING THE ENDS

Your bracelet is long enough when it goes about two-thirds of the way around your wrist. Since this bracelet has six threads, you can make two braids. Each braid uses three threads.

Spread out your three threads. You have one on the left (L), one in the centre (C) and one on the right (R).

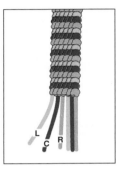

1. L goes over C and becomes the new C.

2. Then R goes over C and becomes the new C. Tighten the threads.

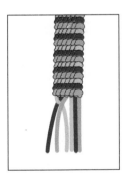

3. Continue L over C then R over C, tightening the threads every now and then to keep the braid even.

4. The braids must be long enough to slip through the loop and tie in a bow. About 7.5 cm (3 inches) works well. Tie an overhand knot in the end of each braid to finish it off. Trim the ends, then slip one braid through the bracelet loop and tie the braids in a bow. You can undo this kind of fastening quite easily.

If you're planning to wear your bracelet until it falls off — in the shower, when you go swimming and when you do the dishes — you can just knot the unbraided ends together. You need the same trimmed 7.5 cm (3 inch) length. Slip three of the loose ends through the loop and knot them around the other three ends.

DIAGONAL STRIPE VARIATION — ZIGZAG BRACELETS

Turn your bracelet over on purpose to get a zigzag effect.

1. Knot three rows, a complete colour pattern, then unpin the bracelet. Turn it over and pin it to your knee again. Now you're looking at the back. You can see that the back looks different from the  front. The front of your bracelet has rows of single stitches. On the back, you can see the two knots that make each stitch.

2. When you've turned your bracelet over, start knotting from the left as usual. You'll repeat the colour of the row you've just finished knotting. Thread 6 becomes thread 1 when you flip the bracelet over. Knot three rows, one of each colour, then turn the bracelet over again.

3. Continue knotting and flipping every three rows until your bracelet is long enough. Then finish it off as usual by braiding the ends.

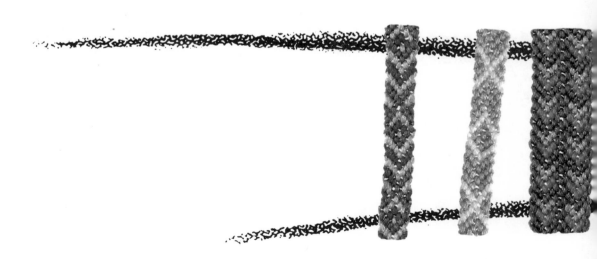

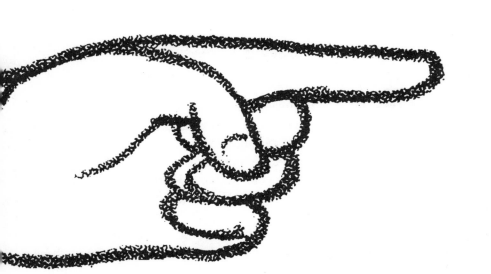

ARROWHEAD BRACELETS

Choose four different colours for this bracelet. Measure your colours as you did for the Diagonal Stripe bracelet (see page 6). Tie the overhand knot to make the loop and pin the bracelet.

This bracelet has an imaginary centre line. You arrange half of the threads on one side of the line and the other half of the threads in a mirror-image pattern on the other.

1. Separate out four threads, one of each colour. Decide which colours you want next to each other in the knotting order and arrange your four threads, untangling them to the ends and fanning them out.

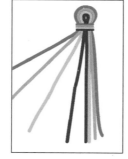

2. Arrange the remaining four threads in a mirror-image pattern. Work in from the outside making sure that the pairs of threads match. Threads 1 and 8 are the same colour, so are 2 and 7, 3 and 6 and 4 and 5.

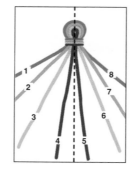

Threads 4 and 5 are side by side, one on each side of the imaginary centre line.

3. Separate out threads 1 to 4, your working threads. They're the threads to the left of the centre line. Put the other threads aside. Now make two knots with thread 1 around threads 2, 3 and 4, and stop. Your knotting thread has travelled halfway across the bracelet to the centre. Put aside those working threads and spread out the threads to the right of the centre line.

4. When you knot from the right side to the centre, your knotting thread travels from right to left. To knot from right to left, pick up the knotting thread — number 8 — with your left hand. Hold the base thread — number 7 — with your right hand,

leaving the right index finger and thumb free to hold the sail shape as it crosses over the base thread. The sail shape points to the right and looks like this.

5. Feed the end of the knotting thread up through the sail shape and pull the knot tight. Make one more knot with thread 8 around thread 7 to complete one stitch.

6. Knot thread 8 twice around threads 6 and 5.

NOTE: The two knotting threads, one that has travelled from the left and one that has travelled from the right, meet in the centre. They are the same colour, and now that they are in the centre of the bracelet they are threads 4 and 5.

7. Since you are moving right to left, make the knots that join the sides of the pattern left-travelling knots. So knot thread 5 twice around thread 4. Pull these joining knots a little tighter than usual as you are pulling together the two halves of the Arrowhead pattern.

8. To continue, knot the new number 1 thread twice around threads 2, 3 and 4, travelling right.

9. Knot the new number 8 thread twice around threads 7, 6 and 5, travelling left.

10. Knot the new centre threads, threads 5 and 4, together with two left-travelling knots. Pull tightly to join the two sides of the pattern.

11. When your bracelet is long enough, you can braid or knot the ends as usual. Make four ends into three groups for braiding by giving one group two ends. The centre can have two threads, with one thread on each side. Braid (see page 11) and knot the ends.

ARROWHEADS WITH A BORDER

The basic Arrowhead pattern organizes the threads and keeps them separate. That's why most bracelets begin with one complete colour pattern of arrowheads — one row knotted in each of the bracelet's colours. The variation begins when the colour pattern repeats itself.

Choose four colours. Measure and set up in the Arrowhead mirror-image colour pattern. Threads 1 and 8 will be the ones used for the border, so remember this when you arrange your colours.

1. Knot one arrowhead in each of the bracelet's four colours.

To begin the variation, you must learn a turnaround stitch that puts the knotting thread right back where it started. A turnaround stitch with thread number 1 is made up of one right-travelling knot and one left-travelling knot. The knotting thread moves over towards the right as it makes its first knot around thread 2, then moves back out to the border because the second knot travels towards the left.

A turnaround stitch with thread 8 around thread 7 is made up of one left-travelling knot that takes the thread in a step, and one right-travelling knot that takes the knotting thread back out to its border.

These stitches are tricky to learn at first because the knotting thread changes hands in the middle of a stitch.

2. Now you can begin the border Arrowhead pattern. With thread 1, knot a turnaround stitch (right-travelling, left-travelling) around thread 2.

3. With thread 8, knot a turnaround stitch (left-travelling, right-travelling) around thread 7. You've knotted the borders for this row. Put the border threads (1 and 8) aside. You'll knot a regular arrowhead with threads 2, 3, 4, 5, 6 and 7.

4. Separate out your working threads 2, 3, 4. Knot thread 2 twice around threads 3 and 4.

5. Separate out your working threads 7, 6 and 5. Knot thread 7 twice around threads 6 and 5.

6. Knot the knotting threads, now threads 5 and 4, together in the centre. Knot thread 5 twice around thread 4.

Each row begins with two turnaround stitches, one on the left border and one on the right border, using threads 1 and 8 as the knotting threads. Threads 2 and 7 are always the knotting threads for the sides of the Arrowhead pattern. Join the sides of the pattern by knotting thread 5 twice around thread 4 as usual.

7. You can finish your bracelet with four rows — one complete colour pattern — of ordinary arrowheads so that the end of your bracelet matches the beginning.

ARROWHEADS WITH A BORDER — COLOUR VARIATIONS

If you measure two lengths of each of two colours and so have four working threads of each colour instead of two, your pattern of arrowheads and border will be different. Every three rows, there will be an arrowhead the same colour as your border.

Arrange your colours in a mirror-image pattern. Threads 1 and 2 and 7 and 8 will be the same colour. Threads 3, 4, 5 and 6 will also be the same colour.

1. Begin as usual with one full colour pattern (four rows) of ordinary arrowheads.

2. Knot the borders as usual: thread 1 knots a right-travelling/left-travelling turnaround stitch around thread 2, and thread 8 knots a left-travelling/right-travelling turnaround stitch around thread 7.

3. Complete the arrowhead using threads 2 and 7 as the knotting threads. The colours, not the knotting pattern, make the bracelet look different.

It's always more difficult to work with several threads of the same colour. Always separate out the working threads and put aside those you have finished with. The border threads always stay at the edges of the bracelet. The arrowheads are always knotted with threads 2 and 7, even when they are the same colour as the borders.

PLAYING WITH COLOURS

Each arrowhead in a pattern is usually knotted with two threads of the same colour — they travel from the outside edges of the bracelet, in opposite directions, then are knotted together when they meet in the centre.

To make a Striped Arrowhead bracelet, you knot arrowheads that are half one colour and half another, using a turnaround stitch where the threads meet in the centre to keep each colour on its own side. You can make an Alternating Arrowhead bracelet if you join the arrowheads in the usual way, with a left-travelling stitch. The arrowhead colours will change sides every four rows — after each complete colour pattern. It's the colour set-up that makes the difference.

STRIPED ARROWHEADS

Choose two colours and measure two lengths of each so that you have four working threads of each of two colours. Set up as usual, with loop, knot and pin.

1. Spread out the four threads of one colour on the left side and the four threads of the other colour on the right side.

2. Begin to knot your first arrowhead. Knot thread 1 twice around threads 2, 3 and 4. All these threads are the same colour, so keep your knotting thread in your right hand. Don't let it go until you've finished knotting the first half of the arrowhead.

3. Start from the right side and knot thread 8 twice around threads 7, 6 and 5. All these threads are the same colour too, so always keep your knotting thread in your left hand.

4. The two knotting threads of different colours meet in the centre. Do a left-travelling/right-travelling turnaround stitch with thread 5 around thread 4 so that each colour stays on its own side of the imaginary centre line.

5. Continue to knot each row, following steps 2, 3 and 4.

ALTERNATING ARROWHEADS

Measure, set up and arrange your colours as you did for the Striped Arrowhead bracelet. Knot your arrowheads in the usual way, joining them with two left-travelling knots. The two colours of the arrowheads will change sides each complete colour pattern (every four rows). Remember that the colour of the knotting thread is the colour of the stitch, so always knot your centre joining stitch the same way — either left-travelling or right-travelling — to keep the colour pattern even.

ARROWHEAD BRACELETS: DOUBLING UP

You can start two Arrowhead bracelets, then join them together after you've knotted one full colour pattern on each one.

There are lots of possible colour patterns. If you start with two identical bracelets, then the same colour pattern will zigzag across the bracelet from one edge to the other. Experiment with different colours.

Set up two identical arrowhead bracelets, and pin them side by side on your working surface. Make sure the loops are about the same size. Decide on the arrangement of your colours, and arrange the threads of the bracelet on the left. This is bracelet number 1.

1. Work one complete colour pattern of arrowheads on bracelet number 1. If you're working with four colours, one colour pattern will be four rows.

2. Arrange the colours of bracelet number 2 — the one on the right. If you didn't write down the colour order, look at the stripes on bracelet 1. Threads 1 and 8 are the colour of row 1; 2 and 7 the colour of row 2; 3 and 6 the colour of row 3; and 4 and 5 the colour of row 4.

3. Work one complete colour pattern of arrowheads on bracelet number 2. The bracelets should now look exactly the same.

4. To join the two bracelets together, knot thread 8 of bracelet 1 twice around thread 1 of bracelet 2. The joining stitch pulls the two bracelets firmly together. The threads of the joining stitch are the same colour.

The joining stitch threads are often hard to find as they're in the very middle of the bracelet. Look at the colour of the row you've just finished, then look near the centre for the two threads of the next colour in your colour pattern. It's helpful to flip all the other threads out of the way while you knot these two threads tightly together.

NOTE: If your bracelets are different colours, the stitch that joins the bracelets together must be the same turnaround stitch — either left-travelling/right-travelling or right-travelling/left-travelling — so that the colours for each bracelet stay on their own sides.

As you continue, you will still work each bracelet separately — then you'll join them together with a stitch at the beginning of each row. Since you're working with 16 threads, be sure to separate out the four threads you need for each part of the pattern. Always put the other threads aside.

5. Flip up all the threads of bracelet 2 so they are out of the way.

6. Begin the Arrowhead pattern working with threads 1 to 4 of bracelet 1. Put aside threads 5 to 8.

7. Now put aside threads 1 to 4. Finish the arrowhead pattern using threads 8 to 5. Join the two sides of the arrowhead by knotting thread 5 twice around thread 4. Remember to pull the knots of the joining stitch tightly together.

8. Put aside all the threads of bracelet 1.

9. Begin the Arrowhead pattern on bracelet 2 as you did with bracelet 1, using threads 1-4.

10. Complete the arrowhead with threads 8 to 5, then join the sides of the arrowhead by knotting thread 5 twice around thread 4. The arrowhead pattern now zigzags in a W shape across the whole bracelet.

11. Begin the next row with a right-travelling joining stitch. Knot thread 8 of bracelet 1 twice around thread 1 of bracelet 2.

DOUBLE ARROWHEADS WITH A BORDER

Arrange your colours as you did for the Double Arrowhead pattern — two matching colour arrangements in a mirror-image set-up.

Begin by working one complete colour pattern of arrowheads on each set of threads.

Remember to always separate out the small group of threads you are working with and put all the other threads aside. As the patterns become more complicated, this way of separating out the working threads will stop you from getting mixed up.

1. Begin with a joining stitch. Knot thread 8 of bracelet 1 twice around thread 1 of bracelet 2. If the two bracelets are identical, this stitch is a regular stitch. If the bracelets are different, this stitch is a turnaround stitch.

2. Work with bracelet 1. Put aside the threads of bracelet 2.

3. Do a right-travelling/left-travelling turnaround border stitch with knotting thread 1 around thread 2. Then do a left-travelling/right-travelling turnaround border stitch with knotting thread 8 around thread 7. Put aside threads 1 and 8.

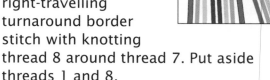

4. Do an arrowhead, knotting thread 2 twice around threads 3 and 4, and thread 7 twice around threads 6 and 5. Join the sides of the Arrowhead pattern together by knotting thread 5 twice around thread 4.

5. Put aside the threads of bracelet 1. Now repeat steps 3 and 4 with the threads of bracelet 2.

6. Begin your next full row with a joining stitch that joins the two bracelets together. Knot thread 8 of bracelet 1 twice around thread 1 of bracelet 2.

DOUBLE BRACELETS WITH SPLIT COLOUR ARROWHEADS

When your colour arrangement is not mirror image but split colour, R/R/R/R/B/B/B/B/R/R/R/R/B/B/B/B, work one pattern on each bracelet until all the threads of each colour have changed sides.

When you join bracelet 1 to bracelet 2 at the beginning of each row, do a turnaround joining stitch. Make sure that this turnaround joining stitch is always the same left-travelling/right-travelling or right-travelling/left-travelling because the stitch is always the colour of the knotting thread.

ZIGZAG Y BRACELETS

Choose four colours. Measure the threads, make a loop and pin as usual. Arrange the colours in a mirror-image set-up. The colour in the centre, threads 4 and 5, will be the colour of the Zigzag Y pattern.

1. Work one complete colour pattern (4 rows) of arrowheads.

2. Now you'll fill in one half of the arrowhead so that a diagonal can run across the bracelet from right to left. First, separate out threads 1 to 3. Then knot thread 1 twice around threads 2 and 3. Knot the new thread 1 twice around thread 2. Now knot thread 4 twice around threads 3, 2 and 1 to complete the first Y.

3. Working right to left, knot thread 8 twice around threads 7, 6, 5, 4, 3 and 2. Don't knot it around the knotting thread of the last row, thread 1.

A full diagonal row has seven stitches. This row has six stitches and each row from now on will have one stitch less.

You never knot around the knotting thread from the last row.

As you finish each row, put the knotting thread aside.

4. Working right to left, knot thread 8 twice around threads 7, 6, 5, 4 and 3. Threads 2 and 1 are the knotting threads from the previous rows. Don't knot around them.

5. Working right to left, knot thread 8 twice around threads 7, 6, 5 and 4. Threads 3, 2 and 1 are the knotting threads from the previous rows. Don't knot around them.

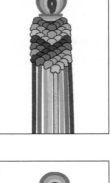

6. Working right to left, knot thread 8 twice around threads 7, 6 and 5. Threads 4, 3, 2 and 1 are the knotting threads from the previous rows. Don't knot around them.

7. Working right to left, knot thread 8 twice around threads 7 and 6.

8. Working right to left, knot thread 8 twice around thread 7.

9. To knot a full diagonal from left to right, knot thread 1 twice around threads 2, 3, 4, 5, 6, 7 and 8. You've completed your second Y. Put the knotting thread aside.

NOTE: Keep an eye on the length of the zigzag Y thread. You're using it more as a knotting thread so it'll get shorter faster than all the other threads.

You worked your first set of diagonals from right to left. This set goes the opposite way — you work from left to right.

1. Knot thread 1 twice around threads 2, 3, 4, 5, 6 and 7. Don't knot it around thread 8, the knotting thread of the last row. Put the knotting thread aside.

2. Knot thread 1 twice around threads 2, 3, 4, 5 and 6. Don't knot around threads 7 and 8, the knotting threads of the last two rows. Put the knotting thread aside.

3. Knot thread 1 twice around threads 2, 3, 4 and 5. Don't knot around threads 6, 7 and 8. Put the knotting thread aside.

4. Knot thread 1 twice around threads 2, 3 and 4. Don't knot around threads 5, 6, 7 and 8. Put the knotting thread aside.

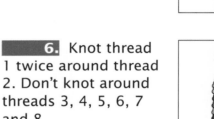

5. Knot thread 1 twice around threads 2 and 3. Don't knot around threads 4, 5, 6, 7 and 8. Put the knotting thread aside.

6. Knot thread 1 twice around thread 2. Don't knot around threads 3, 4, 5, 6, 7 and 8.

7. You've finished the fill-in. Now knot a full diagonal from right to left. Knot thread 8 twice around threads 7, 6, 5, 4, 3, 2 and 1.

8. Continue filling in. The diagonals will alternate as you work right to left, then left to right. Six or seven Zigzag Y patterns make a good bracelet.

9. When you want to stop, make an X pattern so that you will have two groups of threads to braid as you finish off your bracelet.

You must begin with a full diagonal row. If your diagonal runs down from right to left, fill in to make the X this way:

a. Knot thread 8 twice around threads 7 and 6.

b. Knot thread 8 twice around thread 7.

c. Knot thread 5 twice around threads 6, 7 and 8.

If your diagonal runs down from left to right:

a. Knot thread 1 twice around threads 2 and 3.

b. Knot thread 1 twice around thread 2.

c. Knot thread 4 twice around threads 3, 2 and 1.

10. Now finish off your bracelet by braiding the ends the usual way.

DIAMONDS AND X'S

Choose four colours of thread. Measure, make a loop and pin your bracelet as usual. Arrange your colours in a mirror-image set-up.

1. Knot one complete colour pattern (four rows) of arrowheads. The last arrowhead of the colour pattern is the top half of the X. As you begin to knot the X and the diamond, remember to pull all the knots firmly in order to keep the pattern together.

To fill in the left side of the X:

2. Knot thread 1 twice around threads 2 and 3.

3. Knot thread 1 twice around thread 2.

4. Knot thread 4 twice around threads 3, 2 and 1 to complete one side of the X.

To fill in the right side of the X:

5. Knot thread 8 twice around threads 7 and 6.

6. Knot thread 8 twice around thread 7.

7. To complete the X, knot thread 5 twice around threads 6, 7 and 8.

To make the first diamond:

8. Put aside threads 1 and 8. You won't be knotting with them yet. When you make the diamond, you work from the centre out to the edges with each colour. You don't knot around the knotting thread of the last row.

9. Knot thread 4 twice around thread 5.

10. Knot thread 4 twice around threads 3 and 2.

11. Knot thread 5 twice around threads 6 and 7. Put aside the knotting threads.

To start a new row:

12. Knot thread 4 twice around thread 5.

13. Knot thread 4 twice around thread 3.

14. Knot thread 5 twice around thread 6. Put aside the knotting threads.

15. Now knot thread 4 twice around thread 5.

16. To complete the left side of the diamond, knot thread 1 twice around threads 2, 3 and 4.

17. To complete the right side of the diamond, knot thread 8 twice around threads 7, 6 and 5.

18. Finish off the diamond by knotting thread 5 twice around thread 4.

You've made an X and Diamond block. You can repeat the plain Arrowhead pattern, followed by the X and Diamond block, or begin to knot another X and Diamond combination by filling in the left side of the X (step 2).

19. If you like, you can finish off this bracelet with one plain set of arrowheads, before braiding the ends as usual.

X'S AND O'S:
A DIAMOND PATTERN
COLOUR VARIATION

The X's in this pattern are real X's, but the O's are diamonds.

Choose two colours of thread and measure only one length of one colour, but three lengths of the other. You will have eight knotting ends, two of one colour, six of the other. Make a loop and pin your bracelet to your working surface as usual.

Arrange the threads in a mirror-image set-up. Threads 4 and 5 will be one colour. Threads 1, 2 and 3 and 6, 7 and 8 will be the other colour.

1. Knot one complete colour pattern (four rows) of arrowheads. The last row of arrowheads is the top half of the first X.

To fill in the left side of the X:

2. Knot thread 1 twice around threads 2 and 3.
3. Knot thread 1 twice around thread 2.
4. Knot thread 4 twice around threads 3, 2 and 1 to complete this part of the X.

To fill in the right side of the X:

5. Knot thread 8 twice around threads 7 and 6.

6. Knot thread 8 twice around thread 7.

7. Knot thread 5 twice around threads 6, 7 and 8 to complete the right side of the X.

Next, you fill in the X with upside-down arrowheads. You knot as you do for the diamond, but each row goes out to the edge.

8. Knot thread 4 twice around thread 5.

9. Then knot thread 4 twice around threads 3, 2 and 1.

10. Knot thread 5 twice around threads 6, 7 and 8.

11. You've completed one row of upside-down arrowheads. Knot three more rows just like this. The last row is the colour of the X. It's the first row of the diamond.

To knot the diamond:

12. Knot thread 4 twice around thread 5.

13. Knot thread 4 twice around threads 3 and 2.

14. Knot thread 5 twice around threads 6 and 7.

15. Knot thread 4 twice around thread 5.

16. Knot thread 4 twice around thread 3, and thread 5 twice around thread 6.

17. Knot thread 4 twice around thread 5.

18. To complete the diamond, knot thread 1 twice around threads 2, 3 and 4 and knot thread 8 twice around threads 7, 6 and 5. Then knot thread 5 twice around thread 4.

19. Knot one complete colour pattern of regular arrowheads. The last arrowhead is the top half of the next X.

DOUBLE DIAMOND BRACELETS

A bracelet in this beautiful pattern will take longer than one sitting to complete, but it's well worth the effort.

Choose four colours, and measure enough thread for two identical bracelets. One of the colours will outline the diamonds and so will get used up faster than the others. Decide on your outline colour and make these lengths of thread one fingertip-to-elbow length longer than the others. Make the loops, and pin the bracelets side by side.

Begin with bracelet 1. Arrange the colours in a mirror-image set-up. The colour you put on the outsides of your mirror-image set-up (the colour of the first arrowhead you knot) will be the colour that outlines your diamonds in the pattern.

1. Knot one complete colour pattern of arrowheads with the threads of bracelet 1.

2. Arrange the threads of bracelet 2, then knot one complete colour pattern of arrowheads with the threads of bracelet 2. Bracelet 1 and bracelet 2 should now look exactly the same.

3. Begin the next row by joining the bracelets together. Knot thread 8 of bracelet 1 twice around thread 1 of bracelet 2.

4. Now that you have joined your bracelets, number your threads 1 to 16. Knot one more complete row of arrowheads that zigzags across your bracelet from left to right. This colour will outline the diamond pattern.

5. Put aside threads 1 to 4 and threads 13 to 16.

To knot a central diamond using threads 5 to 12:

Remember that you don't knot around the knotting threads of the previous row.

6. Knot thread 8 twice around thread 9.

7. Knot thread 8 twice around threads 7 and 6.

8. Knot thread 9 twice around threads 10 and 11.

9. Knot thread 8 twice around thread 9.

10. Knot thread 8 twice around thread 7.

11. Knot thread 9 twice around thread 10.

12. Knot thread 8 twice around thread 9.

13. Complete the diamond by knotting thread 5 twice around threads 6, 7 and 8, and thread 12 twice around threads 11, 10 and 9.

14. Knot thread 9 twice around thread 8.

Look at your threads. There are three threads, then a thread that's the colour of the Diamond pattern outline. Three more threads, then two threads that are the colour of the outline. Three more threads, then an outline thread, and three more threads. The outline threads divide the other threads into groups. As you work, always remember to separate out your groups of working threads. Put all the other threads aside. Remember also to pull firmly on the threads as you tie your knots to keep all the pieces of the pattern together.

The next pattern block has two diamonds.

To fill in the outside edges and finish off two X's:

15. Knot thread 1 twice around threads 2 and 3.

16. Knot thread 1 twice around thread 2.

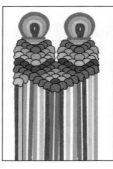

17. Knot thread 4 twice around threads 3, 2 and 1. You've completed the X on the left side of your bracelet.

18. Knot thread 16 twice around threads 15 and 14.

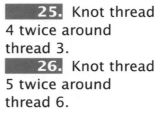

19. Knot thread 16 twice around thread 15.

20. Knot thread 13 twice around threads 14, 15 and 16. You've completed the X on the right side of your bracelet.

The first diamond is knotted with threads 1 to 8.

21. Knot thread 4 twice around thread 5.

22. Knot thread 4 twice around threads 3 and 2.

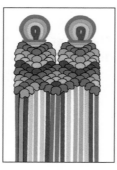

23. Knot thread 5 twice around threads 6 and 7.

24. Knot thread 4 twice around thread 5.

25. Knot thread 4 twice around thread 3.

26. Knot thread 5 twice around thread 6.

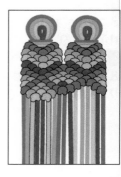

27. Knot thread 4 twice around thread 5.

28. To complete the diamond, knot thread 1 twice around threads 2, 3 and 4, and knot thread 8 twice around threads 7, 6 and 5. Knot thread 5 twice around thread 4.

The second diamond is knotted with threads 9 to 16:

29. Knot thread 12 twice around thread 13.

30. Knot thread 12 twice around threads 11 and 10.

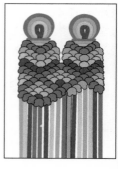

31. Knot thread 13 twice around threads 14 and 15.

32. Knot thread 12 twice around thread 13.

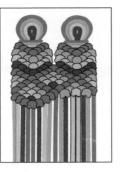

33. Knot thread 12 twice around thread 11.

34. Knot thread 13 twice around thread 14.

35. Knot thread 12 twice around thread 13.

36. Complete the diamond by knotting thread 9 twice around threads 10, 11 and 12, and thread 16 twice around threads 15, 14 and 13. Knot thread 13 twice around thread 12.

37. Now you're ready to repeat the pattern by knotting another central diamond as you did in the first block. These are the steps of the pattern: Knot a central diamond. Fill in the sides of the pattern to complete two X's, then knot two diamonds.

SKINNY BRACELETS

You can make different kinds of Skinny Bracelets, using one, two, three or four colours. If you begin your bracelet with a loop, choose two colours and measure them as usual. Make a loop with a knot and pin the bracelet to your working surface.

If you want to use up some ends of skeins, you can use several different colours. You always work with four knotting threads. It's best if each thread is about an arm's length. Put one end of each of the threads together, and tie an overhand knot. Be sure to leave tag ends of 7 to 10 cm (3 to 4 inches), so that you can tie the bracelet onto your wrist.

You can combine three kinds of patterns in your Skinny Bracelets. The first gives you a spiral twist of stitches. The second gives you a straight row of stitches, and the third gives you a row of flowers. You can mix and match the blocks until your bracelet is long enough.

THE SPIRAL TWIST

You have four working threads. Three will be the core, while the fourth is the knotting thread. When you've knotted a long enough block of stitches, the knotting thread returns to the core, and one of the core threads becomes the knotting thread.

1. Choose the knotting thread. Your first block of stitches will be this colour. It is thread 1. Threads 2, 3 and 4 are the core threads. Think of them as only one thread as you'll knot thread 1 around them all.

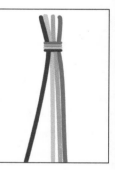

2. Knot thread 1 around threads (2, 3, 4) with a right-travelling knot. Do two more right-travelling knots. You'll see that the knots are starting to spiral over towards the right. Do some more right-travelling knots. The knotting thread travels all the way across the bracelet to the right side.

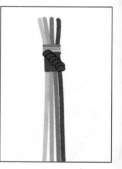

3. Flip the knotting thread underneath the core threads and bring it out on the left side of the bracelet again. Now begin knotting again, still using right-travelling knots.

With this pattern, it's easier to count single knots rather than stitches when you are making your blocks of pattern. Twenty or twenty-five single right-travelling knots should give you about three spirals.

4. Return the knotting thread to the core. Choose a different colour this time. You want to use up different threads when you knot. Knot more spirals, or choose a different pattern.

THE STRAIGHT STITCH

If you do a right-travelling knot followed by a left-travelling knot, followed by another right-travelling knot, then one more left-travelling knot, you will end up with a straight row of stitches. You're actually making one turn-around stitch on top of the other. Count 20 or 25 knots to make your next block, and return the knotting thread to the core.

Choose your next knotting thread. If you're making spirals or straight rows, choose a thread that you haven't already used as a knotting thread. You want to use up all the threads evenly. You can choose to knot a block of flowers.

FLOWERS

To make a flower, spread out your threads. They're numbered 1 to 4. Threads 2 and 3 should be the same colour. You will knot the flower with them. Threads 1 and 4 are also the same colour.

1. Knot thread 2 twice around thread 3.

2. Knot thread 2 twice around thread 1.

3. Knot thread 3 twice around thread 4.

4. Knot thread 2 twice around thread 3. This is the centre of the flower.

5. Knot thread 1 twice around thread 2.

6. Knot thread 4 twice around thread 3.

7. Now knot thread 3 twice around thread 2 to complete one flower.

To move right on to the next flower:

8. Knot thread 2 twice around thread 1.

9. Knot thread 3 twice around thread 4.

10. Knot thread 2 twice around thread 3.

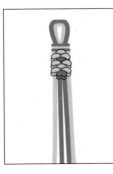

11. Knot thread 1 twice around thread 2.

12. Knot thread 4 twice around thread 3.

13. Knot thread 3 twice around thread 2 to complete your second flower.

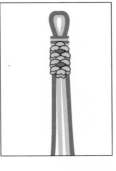

14. Continue on from step 8 to make more flowers. Three or four flowers make a nice-sized block.

FLOWER HINTS:

Since skinny bracelets flip over easily, be careful that you don't mix up the front and the back of your flower. Your pairs of knotting threads may be of unequal length. When you are knotting together two threads of the same colour, use the longer one as the knotting thread.

MIX AND MATCH BRACELETS

You can mix and match pattern blocks to make different kinds of bracelets. Here's an idea that uses arrowheads, X's and diamonds, and spiral twists and straight rows. You'll find the pattern idea here, but not the instructions for each block.

Choose four colours, measure, make a loop and set up your threads. Use a mirror-image colour arrangement.

1. Knot a complete colour pattern of arrowheads. (See page 14.)

2. Fill in and knot the rest of the X. (See page 28.)

3. Knot a diamond. (See page 28.)

4. With thread 1, knot a spiral twist around thread 2 — do about 20 knots. And with thread 8, knot a spiral twist of 20 knots around thread 7. (See page 36.)

5. Knot a straight row of about 20 knots with thread 3 around thread 4, and with thread 6 around thread 5. (See page 37.) The straight rows and the spiral rows should be the same length.

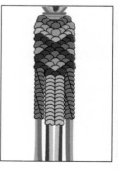

6. Join the pieces of the pattern together by knotting an arrowhead with threads 2 and 7, the same threads you used to knot the spirals.

7. Begin the pattern again by knotting another arrowhead, this time with threads 1 and 8. This arrowhead will be the top half of the next X.

The pattern for the whole bracelet reads like this: Arrowheads, X/Diamond Combination, Spiral Twist/Straight Row Combination, X/Diamond Combination, Spiral Twist/Straight Row Combination, X/Diamond Combination, Arrowheads.

Here's an alternative to the X to bridge arrowheads and spiral twist, straight row, or flower combinations.

Knot your arrowheads as usual.

To fill in the left side:

1. Knot thread 1 twice around threads 2 and 3.
2. Knot thread 1 twice around thread 2.

3. Knot thread 3 twice around threads 2 and 1.
4. Knot thread 4 twice around threads 3, 2 and 1.

To fill in the right side:

5. Knot thread 8 twice around threads 7 and 6.
6. Knot thread 8 twice around thread 7.

7. Knot thread 6 twice around threads 7 and 8.
8. Knot thread 5 twice around threads 6, 7 and 8.

You can follow this fill-in with a row of straight stitches on each edge, and a row of flowers in between.

If you add an extra row of arrowheads after you've knotted together the straight row/flower combination, you'll use up the threads more evenly and vary the colours of your bracelet.

If your last combination is an X or its alternative fill-in, you can finish off the bracelet with a set of upside-down arrowheads. (See page 31.)

ABOUT BEADS

When you're choosing beads, remember that the holes must be big enough for one or two embroidery threads.

If you happen to have a plastic dental floss threader, it's perfect for feeding the threads through the bead. The threader is a long thin piece of plastic that splits into two to make a bendy loop. You just feed the ends of the thread through the loop. It's like threading a needle, but much easier because the loop is so big. Then feed the plastic "needle" part through the hole in the bead.

Beads work well with the arrowhead pattern. You might decide to put in a bead each time you knot a row of a certain colour. You can add a bead when you make the stitch that joins the two sides of the arrowhead together. There are two ways to do it. Try them both to see which you like best.

Make the first of the two knots of the joining stitch. Slip the bead onto the knotting thread. Then complete the stitch by tying one knot with the other thread. Knot the next row as usual, even though it's a stretch to knot around the bead. When you put the bead into the pattern this way, the bead sits above the knotted surface.

If your bead has a hole that's big enough for two threads, slip them both through the bead before you knot the stitch that joins the sides of the arrowhead pattern. When you put the bead into the pattern this way, the bead sits almost level with the knotted surface of the bracelet.

EARRINGS AND THINGS

Earrings and key chains are a great way to use up left-over bits and pieces, especially if you add beads.

Knot two colour patterns — eight rows — of arrowheads. Slip a bead into the pattern after the first four rows. Trim the ends to make a fringe or add more beads. Or make a loop, then knot four spiral twists and tie a bead onto the end of each one.

Use the Single or Double Diamonds pattern to make earrings or a key chain. Add beads when you knot the single-stitch row of the diamond fill-in — just before you complete the diamond outline.

If you start your work with tag ends and an overhand knot instead of a loop, you'll have fringes at both ends. Make your work long enough to tie around a pony tail or braid.

Once you know some of the basic patterns and blocks, you can combine them in any way you like. Let your imagination go wild — and decorate yourself from head to toe.

READY REFERENCE

THE BASIC KNOT

Your knotting thread can travel in different directions.

The knotting thread is travelling from left to right.

To make a knot you:

1. Hold the knotting thread in your right hand.

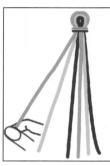

2. Pick up the base thread with the middle, ring and little fingers of your left hand. Leave your left thumb and index finger free.

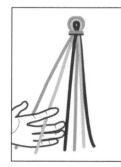

3. Make a sail shape with your knotting thread. The sail shape points to the left and looks like this.

The sail thread crosses over the base thread. Your left index finger and thumb hold the threads together where they cross.

4. Feed the end of the knotting thread up through the sail shape. Hold the base thread tight and straight and pull the knot up to the top of the base thread.

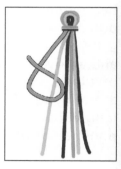

TWO KNOTS ON A BASE THREAD MAKE A STITCH.

This is how you make an ordinary stitch when the knotting thread is travelling towards the right.

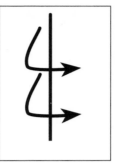

TWO KNOTS ON A BASE THREAD MAKE A STITCH.

This is how you make an ordinary stitch when the knotting thread is travelling towards the left.

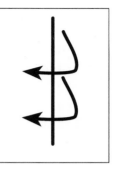

The knotting thread is travelling from right to left.

To make a knot you:

1. Pick up the knotting thread with your left hand.

2. Hold the base thread with your right hand.

3. Make a sail shape with the knotting thread. The sail shape points to the right and looks like this.

4. Your right index finger and thumb hold the sail thread where it crosses over the base thread. Feed the end of the knotting thread up through the sail shape. Hold the base thread tight and straight and pull the knot up to the top of the base thread.

Sometimes a thread travels one step over as it knots around a thread, then returns to its place as the stitch is completed on the thread. These stitches are called turnaround stitches. There are two kinds of turnaround stitches, right-travelling/left-travelling and left-travelling/right-travelling.

Turnaround stitches can be tricky until you get used to them because the knotting thread changes hands in the middle of the stitch.

A right-travelling/left-travelling turnaround stitch has one knot that travels towards the right followed by one that travels towards the left.

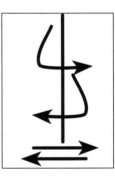

A left-travelling/right-travelling turnaround stitch has one knot that travels towards the left followed by one that travels towards the right.

A split-colour set-up using purple and yellow threads looks like this:

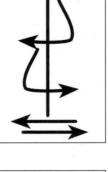

An alternating colour set-up with purple, yellow, blue and green threads looks like this:

You can knot travelling left towards the centre. The stitches look like this:

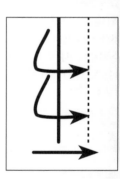

A mirror-image colour set-up with purple, yellow, blue and green threads looks like this:

You can knot travelling right towards the centre. The stitches look like this:

You can knot from the centre travelling left. The stitches look like this:

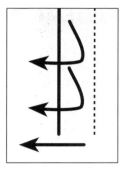

You can knot travelling left towards the centre, then turn around (left-travelling/right travelling turnaround). The stitches look like this:

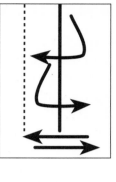

You can knot from the centre travelling right. The stitches look like this:

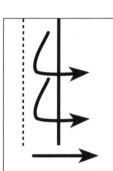

You can knot from the centre travelling left then turn around (left-travelling/right-travelling turnaround). The stitches look like this:

You can knot travelling right towards the centre, then turn around (right-travelling/left-travelling turnaround). The stitches look like this:

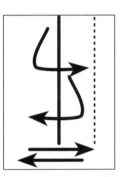

You can knot from the centre travelling right then turn around (right-travelling/left-travelling turnaround). The stitches look like this:

WHAT IF I MAKE A MISTAKE?

How do I undo mistakes?
Stitches are easier to undo from the back because you can see both of the knots that make up each stitch. Use a safety pin to loosen each knot, then undo it with your fingers.

Help! I have a tangle.
To unravel tangled threads, pull out just one thread at a time.

One stitch is the wrong colour. What happened?
Each stitch should be the colour of the knotting thread. If you don't hold the base thread tight, your stitch may be the colour of the base thread instead. Sometimes you can fix it by tugging on the base thread. Sometimes you must undo the stitch, then re-knot it, keeping the base thread taut.

REMEMBER

- Threads are always numbered from left to right. Thread 1 is always on the left side of the bracelet. Thread 8 (or 16) is always on the right. The threads take their names from their positions, so the names of the threads are always changing.

- Don't let your work flip over accidentally. There is always a back and a front. The front is made up of single stitches. On the back you can see the two knots that make up each stitch.

- Always separate out the working threads for each part of the pattern. Put the other threads aside.